Bad Dog, Digby!

North Eastern Educ. and Library Board	
NESPS	
C40 0203666	
Askews	22-Apr-2008
JF	£8.99

Wayland
338 Euston Road
London NW1 3BH

Wayland Australia
Hachette Children's Books
Level 17/207 Kent Street
Sydney, NSW 2000

The rights of Claire Llewellyn to be identified as the Author and Jacqueline East to be identified as the Illustrator of this Work have been asserted by them in accordance with the Copyright, Designs and Patents Act, 1988.

All rights reserved

Series editor: Louise John
Cover design: Paul Cherrill
Design: D.R.ink
Consultant: Shirley Bickler

A CIP catalogue record for this book is available from the British Library.

ISBN 9780750251778 (hbk)

Printed in China

Wayland is a division of Hachette Children's Books, an Hachette Livre UK Company

Bad Dog, Digby!

Written by Claire Llewellyn
Illustrated by Jacqueline East

WAYLAND

Pip had a dog called Digby.

Sometimes Digby was a good dog, but sometimes he was bad!

Pip and Digby liked to play together.

Sometimes they played with Digby's ball.
"Catch!" said Pip.

Sometimes they played with Digby's bone.
Digby liked this game.

But, one day, Digby
chewed Mum's boots.

Mum was cross.
"Bad dog, Digby!"
she said.

Then Digby ran after the cat. The cat was cross. "Meow!" she said.

The postman came to the house. Digby chewed his shoes.
"Bad dog, Digby!" said Pip.

Then Mum saw Digby playing in the bin.

"Oh, Digby!" said Mum. "What a mess!"

Mum was very cross.
She took Digby upstairs.

"It's time for a wash!"
she said.

Mum put Digby in the bath. Mum and Pip gave him a wash.

Digby was tired.
He fell asleep.

START READING is a series of highly enjoyable books for beginner readers. They have been carefully graded to match the Book Bands widely used in schools. This enables readers to be sure they choose books that match their own reading ability.

The Bands are:

| Pink / Band 1 |
| Red / Band 2 |
| Yellow / Band 3 |
| Blue / Band 4 |
| Green / Band 5 |
| Orange / Band 6 |
| Turquoise / Band 7 |
| Purple / Band 8 |
| Gold / Band 9 |

START READING books can be read independently or shared with an adult. They promote the enjoyment of reading through satisfying stories supported by fun illustrations.

Claire Llewellyn has written many books for children. Some of them are about real things like animals or the Moon. Others are storybooks, like this one. Claire has two children of her own, but they are getting too big for stories like this. She hopes that you will enjoy reading her stories instead now!

Jacqueline East scratched her first drawing into her mum's sideboard when she was six! She has enjoyed drawing animals ever since and has a naughty dog called Scampi, who often appears in her books! When Jacqueline is not drawing, she likes to dance and play the guitar.